# Emergency Aid at Work

## FOR APPOINTED PERSONS

First published in Great Britain in 1990 by
The Order of St John, Priory House,
St John's Lane, London EC1M 4DA
071–251 2482


First edition September 1990 34/53946

ISBN 0 900 700 51 3
St John Supplies Product R00006

Printed in England by Lamport Gilbert Printers Ltd, Reading

# FOREWORD BY THE DIRECTOR-GENERAL

This short book contains the details of some of the most important skills that you will ever learn, for it could help you to save someone's life.

These techniques are taught by St John Ambulance in a four hour Emergency Aid course. This course is especially recommended for those who are designated by their employers as 'appointed persons' under the Health and Safety (First Aid) Regulations 1981.

Your place of work will be safer for you and your colleagues if, during the vital few minutes after an accident, someone can perform the simple procedures that follow.

Please learn them, revise them and practise them, one day you will be glad that you knew what to do . . .

Thank you for taking the time to find out about Emergency Aid.

ROBERT BALCHIN
*Director-General St John Ambulance*

*I am grateful to Dr Cleon White, Dr Harry Baker, Dr Geoffrey Brown, Dr Chris Lund, Dr Con Molloy, Dr David Zideman, Robert Adamson, Leslie Gibbons, James Cork, who gave up such a great deal of their time to assist me with the preparation of this book.*

*The drawings are by Sally Reason.*

# CONTENTS

This book has been designed for use in three ways:

**1** As basic instruction about Emergency Aid.

**2** As an aid to memory to help you recall key points.

**3** As a quick reference book in an emergency.

**Number 1** means that you have to read through the book carefully, taking time to answer any questions and then to check your answers against those provided.

**Number 2** means that you have to read the book regularly.

**Number 3** means that you always have to keep the book in a handy place and that you know where to find the EMERGENCY INDEX (page 68).

It is hoped that having read the book you will be willing to undergo practical training – details of the courses run by St John Ambulance are on page 67.

## Special terms

The following special terms are employed in this book, they are fully explained in the text but it might be helpful to have a note of them here.

**AIRWAY:** Another name for the windpipe and air passages.

**EXTERNAL CHEST COMPRESSION:** A technique for pumping blood around the body.

**MOUTH-TO-MOUTH BREATHING:** A technique for getting air into the lungs and restarting breathing. In many text books this is referred to as mouth-to-mouth ventilation.

**CAROTID PULSE:** This is the strongest pulse and is located in the neck. It can be found by sliding your finger tips into the hollow between the voice box and the adjoining muscle.

In any place of work there is the chance of an accident – that is why this book has been written. Whether you work on a building site, a farm, or in an office or factory, it is essential that you know the basic life saving skills which are known as "Emergency Aid".

You might think that this topic is someone else's problem – but is it? Accidents don't always happen near that "someone else" and one of your friends or colleagues could die if you do not know what to do. Also in some circumstances, the wrong action could do more harm than good. That is why it is so important that you work through this book carefully, answering all the questions as you go.

Reading this book will not make you a qualified First Aider. It will nevertheless be helpful to you if you are an Appointed Person under the Health and Safety (First Aid) Regulations 1981. At present an Appointed Person is not required by law to undergo First Aid training but it is strongly recommended that you attend a course run by St John Ambulance (see details on page 67).

The next page shows some of the situations in which Appointed Persons are appropriate.

Always remember that you could well be the first at the scene of an accident . . .

*Would you be able to cope?*

"*An employer shall provide, or ensure that there are provided, such equipment and facilities as is adequate and appropriate in the circumstances for rendering first aid to his employees——*".

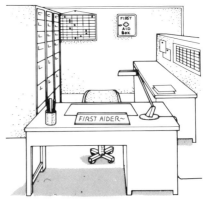

"*An Appointed Person is a person provided by an employer to take charge of the situation – if a serious injury occurs in the absence of a first aider——*".

"*An employer has to provide as a minimum an Appointed Person at all times when employees are at work*".

*The above statements are extracts from or based on the Health and Safety Commission "Approved Code of Practice" for First Aid at Work published by HMSO.*

*When Emergency Aid is required, it is needed very quickly and this section explains why.*

In some ways the body is like a machine – and damage to any of the parts can involve the rest. In particular, if the brain is affected and stops working, then we die. The brain can be damaged directly or from such an injury. If the effect of this is to reduce the supply of oxygen to the brain, its working will be impaired.

Oxygen enters the body when we breathe in air. If the breathing (respiratory) system is damaged so that air does not enter the body the casualty will die. This drawing shows the passages down which air travels to the lungs.

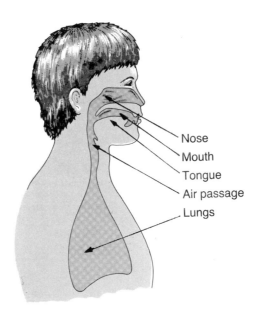

Nose
Mouth
Tongue
Air passage
Lungs

*Fig. 1 – Face and Chest (Section) showing simplified airway*

You will learn more about breathing on page 14.

9

Once the air has reached the lungs, its oxygen must then be carried to the brain (and other parts of the body) – and the blood and the circulatory system do this for us. The oxygen is carried from the lungs in red blood cells. Bright red "oxygenated" blood passes into the heart and is then pumped around the body through blood vessels called arteries. When the oxygen has been used by body tissues the "deoxygenated" blood flows through the veins, to the heart and back to the lungs.

If the blood, carrying oxygen, does not circulate to the brain, then after 3 minutes, brain cells start to die. As a result, the casualty could suffer brain damage or die.

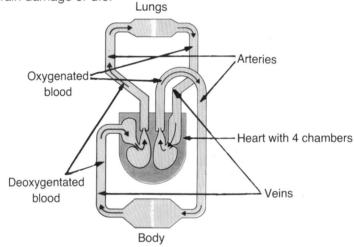

*Fig. 2 – Circulatory System (Simplified)*

More information about circulation will be found on page 27.

If blood is lost (for example through a bad cut) less oxygen can be carried to the brain and other parts of the body. If a large quantity of blood is lost this could lead to death. **Loss of blood also creates the risk of shock** (see page 47).

Some injuries can cause the body to bleed internally, and although the blood is not lost from the body, it is still lost from the circulatory system and cannot carry oxygen to the brain and other parts. Treatments for bleeding from wounds or internal injuries are covered in Chapter Six.

If the brain receives some oxygen (but not enough to work properly), then **unconsciousness** could occur (see page 32).

Throughout this book we will be looking at ways in which you can help in an emergency. You will learn how to cope with all the situations mentioned so far and, in addition, how to help people with other injuries until a qualified First Aider arrives.

We start by remembering these words for they remind you of our standard procedure for Emergency Aid:

**SAFEGUARD**

**EXAMINE**

**EMERGENCY AID**

**MEDICAL HELP**

To help you remember, notice that their initial letters spell **SEEM**.

You should always carry out these 4 steps at any accident . . . but do not waste time!

1 **SAFEGUARD** yourself and others from any danger (after finding out what happened) especially make sure that you do not put yourself at risk by helping.

2 **EXAMINE** the casualty and decide what emergency aid is required.

3 **Give EMERGENCY AID** – read the rest of this book to learn what to do.

4 **Get qualified MEDICAL HELP** if necessary and then report the accident using the standard procedure which operates in your place of work.

In this book you will find questions for you to answer. Some of the examples may not match your own work situation, but **do** answer them. Think about these examples because they will help you to learn about particular points.

*For instance, consider this emergency . . .*

You work in the packing section of a factory – there is a bang and suddenly one of your workmates screams with pain:

**Fig. 3**

Immediately you remember "**SEEM**":

**1 SAFEGUARD:** The case could fall on the casualty. Make the situation safe, secure the case or remove the casualty. The general rule to follow is move the danger, not the casualty.

**2 EXAMINE:** Let us look at the incident a little more closely. You see that the leg is injured and possibly broken.

**3 EMERGENCY AID:** You might be tempted to take your workmate to the First Aid Room and wait for an ambulance – do not do so! It is essential that you do not move a casualty with a serious injury unless life is at risk. In this case, moving the broken leg might cause a much more serious injury, such as damage to a blood vessel or a nerve.

**4 MEDICAL HELP:** It is obvious here that qualified medical help must be called at once. Whilst you are ensuring that the casualty's condition does not worsen, a colleague **must telephone immediately.**

The first EMERGENCY AID techniques that we learn about concern the body's need for oxygen (which we discussed in Chapter 1). There are many potential causes of death including:

- Insufficient oxygen (for example in a smoke filled room).
- The nose, mouth or windpipe (airway) are blocked (for instance by water).
- The blood is chemically poisoned so that it cannot carry the oxygen.
- The heart is not working.
- The lungs are not working because the chest is trapped or damaged.
- The brain or nerves are damaged so that breathing cannot occur.

ANY OF THESE COULD OCCUR IN A WORK SITUATION.

Remember, after 3 minutes from the time breathing ceased, cells in the brain start to die through lack of oxygen and the casualty will suffer brain damage or die.

*So, in the first 3 minutes you must:*

**SAFEGUARD:**      As necessary.

**EXAMINE:**        Check for breathing by placing your face close to the casualty's mouth, looking along the chest and abdomen. You may hear or feel air being breathed out against your face and see the rise and fall of the casualty's chest and abdomen.

**EMERGENCY AID:**  The Emergency Aid if an unconscious casualty is not breathing and his heart has stopped is to get oxygen into his or her lungs and move the blood (carrying this oxygen) around the body to the brain. This is known as the ABC procedure.

                    **A for Airway**
                    **B for Breathing**
                    **C for Circulation**

**MEDICAL HELP:**   Send someone immediately.

Please learn these terms which are explained a little later.

In the majority of cases you might meet, the ABC procedure could save a life.

**Question:** Three minutes can seem quite a long time. If you find someone who is not breathing and know that a more qualified colleague is close, you might choose to fetch him to help. Why would that be the wrong decision? In other words why should you act immediately?

**Answer:** One of the main reasons is that you do not know when the casualty actually stopped breathing. Also it might take you longer than you expect to get help.

## A: AIRWAY

The "A" of ABC stands for AIRWAY, another name for the windpipe and air passages.

If an unconscious casualty is not breathing, what could block the airway? The commonest cause is that the tongue falls to the back of the throat, like this:

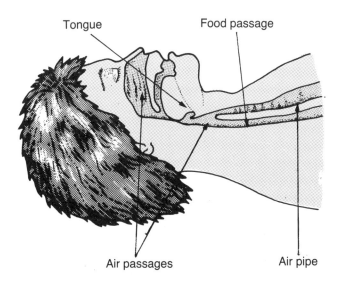

Tongue

Food passage

Air passages

Air pipe

*Fig. 4 – Section of head showing tongue blocking airway.*

*To open the airway:*

Lift the chin forward with the index and middle fingers of one hand while pressing the forehead backward with the heel of the other hand as shown in the diagram below. This will lift the tongue forward, opening the airway like this:

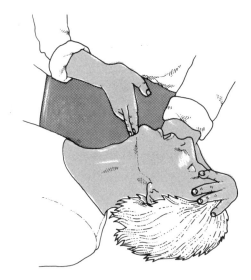

**Fig. 5**

Other causes of blocked airway may be obvious, such as a plastic bag over a child's face, or a large sweet or other object in the mouth. Another possibility is that food that has been vomited lodges in the throat or the back of the mouth.

If you cannot see the obstruction, treat as for choking (pages 24 and 25). Only visible obstructions should be removed, using two fingers to sweep the mouth clear, otherwise there is a danger that the obstruction could be pushed further down the throat.

It is essential to open the airway for anyone who is not breathing – simply doing this could let the casualty breathe for himself . . . and save his life!

## Learning to Restart Breathing

The casualty will die if he or she does not start breathing so you must help by blowing into the casualty's lungs. This technique works because the air that you breathe out contains enough **unused** oxygen to sustain life and you blow that into the casualty's lungs.

The name by which we call this technique is **Mouth-to-Mouth Breathing**.

*If a casualty is not breathing you must:*

● Remove anything external which is obviously in the way.
● Loosen quickly any constrictive clothing etc around the neck.
● Open the airway (page 16).
● Look inside the mouth. If an obstruction is seen, sweep with two fingers to remove it.

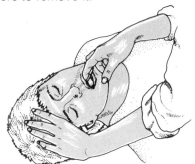

*Fig. 6*

● Open your mouth wide and take a deep breath.
● Pinch the casualty's nostrils together (to stop air escaping).
● Put your lips around the casualty's mouth, making a firm seal.

*Fig. 7*

17

● Blow until you see the casualty's chest rise.

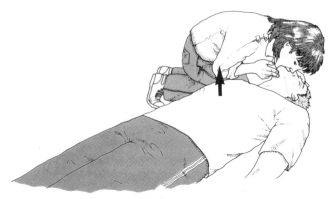

*Fig. 8*

● Move your mouth well away and watch the chest fall.
● Take a deep breath and repeat the process.
● Continue at a rate equal to your normal breathing rate (12/16 breaths per minute for an adult).

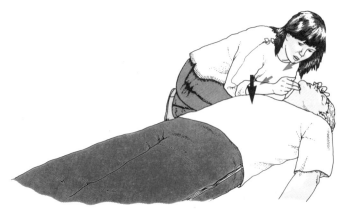

*Fig. 9*

The casualty might start breathing again at any time but may still need to continue Mouth-to-Mouth breathing until his breathing settles into a normal pattern.

*Now think about this question, why do you need to check that the chest has risen?*

*The answer is:*

If the casualty's chest fails to rise, the airway is blocked and you need to clear it. (See choking pages 24 and 25.)

You must keep on breathing for the casualty until qualified help arrives or someone takes over from you. DO NOT GIVE UP! The casualty may recover even after needing a long period of **mouth-to-mouth breathing.** Remember that as long as the heart is beating, the oxygen you are breathing into the casualty will be taken to the brain and body tissues, and his life may be saved.

In the case of a child, you would blow less air into the lungs, and with a baby, a gentle puff is all that is required. Another point when dealing with children, is that you may need to cover the nose and mouth.

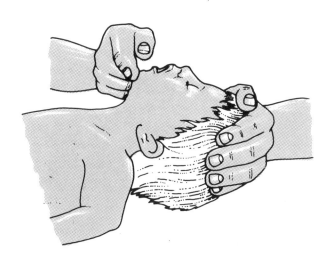

***Fig. 10 – Mouth-to-mouth and nose.***

With anyone who has for example, wounds round the mouth, you may have to close the mouth with your fingers and blow into the casualty's nose. (If you do not block the mouth, your breath will escape instead of going into the casualty's lungs.)

19

## Recovery Position

When the casualty starts breathing, he might remain unconscious and so the tongue could fall to the back of the throat and block the airway, or else the casualty might vomit. In order to ensure that the airway remains open, you should place him in what is known as the **Recovery Position:**

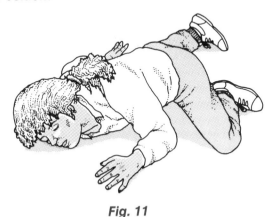

*Fig. 11*

This position lets the casualty breathe easily – but if you look at this diagram you will see other advantages:

*Fig. 12*

*Think about these:*

What happens to the tongue? What will happen to any vomit?

*Answer:*

If the head is tilted back, then the tongue falls clear of the airway. Vomit would run away so that there is no risk of it blocking the airway.

## Learning the Recovery Position.

Let us look in more detail at how we place someone in this position. If a casualty's breathing becomes noisy or difficult, and this is not relieved by opening the airway, or if the person has to be left for a short while, you MUST place them in the recovery position despite any fears about other injuries.

*This is the easiest way to do it:*

1 Kneel upright alongside the casualty, facing his chest, tilting his head back to ensure the airway is open.

2 Place his nearest arm by his side with the palm under the buttocks – palm upwards if possible and making sure the fingers are straight. Bring his forearm over the front of the chest. Holding his far leg under the knee or ankle, bring it towards you and across the near leg.

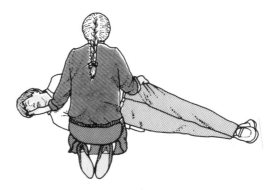

*Fig. 13*

3 Protect and support the casualty's head with one hand, and with the other, grasp the clothing at the hip furthest from you. Pull the casualty towards you and support him against your thighs.

*Fig. 14*

**4** Check and adjust the position of the head to ensure that the airway is open. Bend the uppermost arm to support the upper part of the body. Bend the uppermost knee, to a right angle to bring the thigh well forward and so support the lower body.

**5** Carefully pull the other arm clear of the buttock so that the arm is alongside the body. This will prevent the casualty rolling onto his back.

*Fig. 15*

In the **recovery position,** the casualty should be lying securely with no more than half of his chest in contact with the ground. The head is tilted back and the jaw kept forward to ensure an open airway.

With a heavy casualty, it may be necessary to grasp the clothing at both the hips and shoulders in order to pull him toward you.

There are some general points about the recovery position:

> **1** It is easy once you have practised it a few times.
>
> **2** Lay the casualty on the injured side if there is a chest injury, or there is bleeding from inside the ear.
>
> **3** Remember that you must **always** use the recovery position when you are dealing with an unconscious casualty.
>
> **4** No more than half of the chest should be in contact with the floor.

*Now look at this picture, what should you do?*

*Fig. 16*

*The answers are:*

**SAFEGUARD:** A colleague has fallen into the water and is drowning: make sure that you can reach him safely.

**EXAMINE:** He has stopped breathing.

**EMERGENCY AID:** Open the airway and restart BREATHING with **mouth-to-mouth breathing** as soon as possible; in this case whilst you are still in the water.
Don't waste time trying to get water out of the lungs.
Remember you have 3 minutes in which to do the above.

**MEDICAL HELP:** Do not go yourself, you are needed for the Emergency Aid, send someone if possible.

## Choking

A common problem to do with breathing is choking. *If the casualty is conscious:*

Remove any debris or loose false teeth by sweeping round the casualty's mouth with two fingers. Then encourage her to cough.

If the object isn't dislodged by coughing then help her to bend over with the head lower than the chest. Slap her smartly between the shoulder blades up to four times – use the heel of your hand.

Each slap should be firm enough to dislodge the obstruction. Check the mouth, hook the obstruction out if it is visible.

If you are dealing with a child you should again encourage him to cough. If this does not work, sit down or kneel on one knee with the child, head down, over the other knee. Support the chest with one hand and slap the child on the back four times as before.

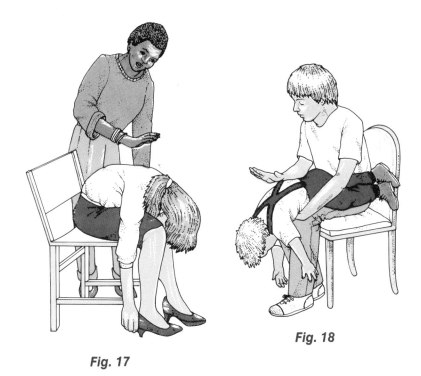

*Fig. 18*

*Fig. 17*

Check the mouth and sweep out the obstruction ONLY IF YOU CAN SEE IT – remember that you must be particularly careful with children that you do **not** push the obstruction down into the airway.

*If the casualty becomes unconscious, what Emergency Aid should you give?*

You should open the airway and apply **mouth-to-mouth breathing** (hopefully, you will be able to blow air past the obstruction and into the casualty's lungs).

If this does not work (if the chest does not rise), pull the casualty onto his side with the chest against your thigh and the head well back (to open the airway). Slap up to four times with the heel of your hand between the shoulder blades. Check the mouth. Keep repeating the process.

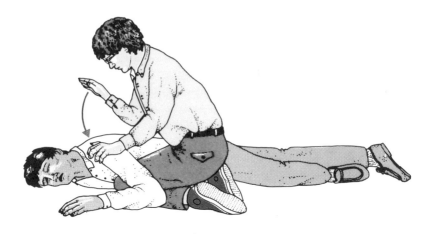

*Fig. 19*

*In this chapter we have covered some major life saving techniques:*

– opening the AIRWAY;
– restarting BREATHING by **mouth-to-mouth breathing**;
– the RECOVERY POSITION;
– how to cope with CHOKING.

**NOTES**

1 Sometimes people feel that mouth-to-mouth contact may be unpleasant. A thin piece of cloth or handkerchief may be placed over the casualty's open mouth before you blow into it. Remember that pausing to do this could waste valuable time and this could result in the casualty's death. You may also be worried about AIDS. You may be reassured to know that no case resulting from mouth-to-mouth breathing has been reported anywhere in the world.

2 You must practice restarting breathing and during a first aid course this is done using a lifelike dummy. **ON NO ACCOUNT PRACTICE ON A BREATHING PERSON.**

Restarting the heart:

We have dealt with A: Airway, B: Breathing. We now turn to C for Circulation.

In this chapter you will learn what to do if a casualty's heart stops beating.

Essential points to note are:

**1** A casualty's heart can be restarted using a technique called external chest compression that will be described shortly.

**2** With it you can force blood carrying oxygen around the body even if the heart has stopped.

**3** If the heart stops then breathing will also stop, so you will have to start it again using **mouth-to-mouth breathing.**

**4** Both techniques (for restarting the heart and for restarting breathing) can be performed at the same time.

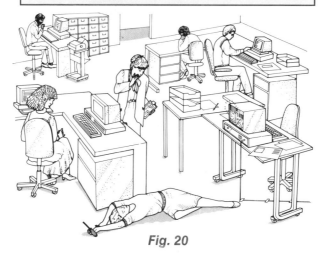

*Fig. 20*

*Look at this picture. What are the first things you would have to do?*

27

**SAFEGUARD:** Is it safe to check her breathing and circulation? No it is not safe! Never risk turning yourself into another casualty. Before you touch her, turn off the power or stand on some dry paper or thick cloth and use, say, a wooden chair to push her away from the electric cable.

**EXAMINE:** The casualty is unconscious and seems to have had an electric shock from a computer terminal.

*You have to check:*

**1** Her breathing (see page 17) and
**2** Whether her heart is beating. To do this you check the pulse.

You may already know how to take the pulse at the wrist . . . but there is a better place to check it. The pulse at the neck (the carotid pulse) is more reliable because it can be felt even if it is very weak.

The carotid pulse is found by sliding your fingers in the hollow between the voice box and the adjoining muscle of the neck.

*Fig. 21*

Try it for yourself. You should find that the heart is beating at a rate between about 60 and 80 per minute. The rate for children is even faster (possibly 100 per minute).

**EMERGENCY AID:** If the heart is not beating. You can keep some blood flowing to vital organs. This carries the oxygen you have breathed into the casualty using **mouth-to-mouth breathing.** You do this by compressing the chest about once per second. However, it is most important that you press in exactly the right place.

The next thing you need to know, therefore, is where to press!

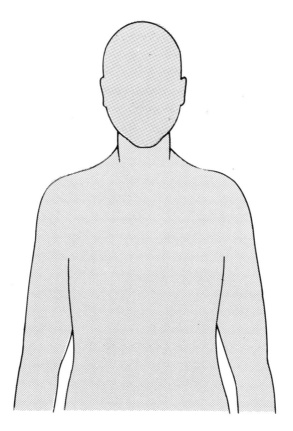

*Fig. 22*

*Look at this drawing and work out where you think you should press.*

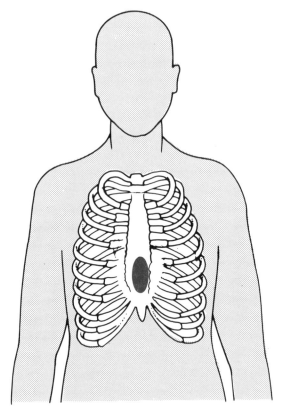

*Fig. 23*

*The position you press is marked.*

If the casualty's heart is not beating you should carry on as follows:

Find the exact spot by putting the heel of your hand three-quarters of the way down the breastbone. (To be precise you should feel where the lower ribs join the breastbone, two finger breadths above this point is where the heel of your hand should go.)

Place the heel of your other hand on top and interlock the fingers, like this:

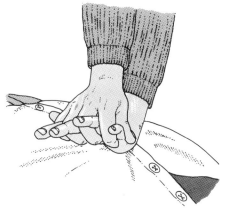

*Fig. 24*

Keep your arm straight and vertical and press the breastbone down about 40–50 mm (1½–2 inches) for an average adult, then release the pressure. Do this at a rate of 80 compressions per minute.

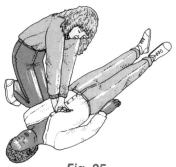

*Fig. 25*

Think about this, should you keep on regularly compressing the chest in this way without doing anything else?

If you carry out **only** these chest compressions then no air will enter the lungs. You must perform a regular cycle of external chest compressions with **mouth-to-mouth breathing**.

For an adult, the cycle is 15 chest compressions followed by two breaths, mouth-to-mouth. You should check the carotid pulse after the initial two breaths, after the first minute and then at three minute intervals.

If there is a second person who is able to give Emergency Aid then the two of you should work as a team – one gives **external chest compressions** at a rate of about 80 times per minute, with a short pause after every five compressions to allow time for the lungs to inflate. The other person keeps the airway open and gives a single inflation of air after every fifth compression.

This technique is hard work but you must not give up! Continue to check the carotid pulse every 3 minutes. When the heartbeat returns then you should stop the chest compressions and just provide **mouth-to-mouth breathing.**

**MEDICAL HELP:** The last stage, as always, is to send for qualified help.

*Now think about this situation:*

**Fig. 26**

You are at a meeting with a colleague when suddenly he goes pale, grasps his chest then slumps to the ground.

*What should you do?*

**SAFEGUARD:**   There is no obvious danger, your colleague appears to have had a heart attack. (See page 62.)

**EXAMINE:**   Is he conscious or unconscious?

If unconscious:

**EMERGENCY AID: You remember ABC AIRWAY, BREATHING, CIRCULATION** .

**Airway:** Open/clear the **AIRWAY** – remove any obvious foreign matter, for example, loose false teeth which might get in the way. Check whether he is breathing (see pages 15 and 16).

**Breathing:** If the casualty is not breathing then:

1 Lay him on his back, flat on the floor.

2 Give 2 deep inflations, mouth-to-mouth.

3 Check whether there is a carotid pulse. If so, carry on with mouth-to-mouth inflation.

**Circulation:** If there is no carotid pulse:

4 Find the junction of the ribs at the bottom of the breastbone. Place the heel of one hand two fingers above this junction.

5 Cover this hand with your other hand.

6 Interlock the fingers (keeping them off the chest so that only the heel of your hand pushes down).

7 Press down with straight arms vertically on the breastbone 4–5 cms and then release.

8 Fifteen external chest compressions should be given (at the rate of 80 per minute).

9 Give 2 deep mouth-to-mouth inflations.

10 Continue to repeat the cycle (15 chest compressions to 2 inflations), checking the carotid pulse after 1 minute and then at 3 minute intervals.

11 If heart beat returns continue inflations at a rate of 12–16 times per minute until normal breathing returns.

12 Place in the **recovery position**. Except for heart attack, on recovery from unconsciousness, keep in the recovery position.

**MEDICAL HELP:**  Finally you must call an ambulance and inform the appropriate people in your organisation. Do not leave the casualty alone or with someone who is unable to give Emergency Aid.

This explanation has been long, but the technique is simple (and remember that if you go on one of the courses mentioned on page 67 you will be able to practice it).

Do not imagine that a heart attack is the only reason for the heart stopping – electric shock, drowning, and a number of other different incidents can create situations in which you may have to save someone's life by using this technique.

In this chapter we will look at the general treatment of unconsciousness which applies to all situations.

*There are many causes of unconsciousness including:*

● Head injury
● Fainting
● Asphyxia (lack of oxygen)
● Heart attack
● Stroke
● Epilepsy
● Diabetes
● Poisoning (including the abuse of alcohol, solvents or drugs).

We normally think of "unconsciousness" as a condition in which the casualty does not react at all. In fact there are varying depths of unconsciousness which can be assessed.

When providing Emergency Aid for the unconscious casualty it is important to carry out the ABC procedures (see page 15) first and then to assess the depth of unconsciousness.

The depth of unconsciousness. This can be based on "shake and shout". Check the casualty in the following way, and make sure that you record the findings together with the time. This must be sent to hospital with the casualty.

---

**1** Is the casualty ALERT, and able to respond with you in a normal way?

**2** Does he respond only to your raised VOICE? This is important as he may be able to give you vital facts about his condition.

**3** Does he only respond to PAIN? You can check this by pinching the back of his hand.

**4** Is he completely UNRESPONSIVE?

---

A note of the changes in the level of responsiveness provide valuable information for the doctors looking after him.

*So check as follows and make a note.*

Remember to check how ALERT he is, whether he responds to your raised VOICE, whether he is unconscious but still responds to PAIN, or whether he is unresponsive.

It is essential that the casualty's condition does not worsen while you are carrying out this assessment. In general, the Emergency Aid for an unconscious person (at whatever level of responsiveness) is to:

> **1** Open the airway.
>
> **2** Check breathing and pulse.
>
> **3** If necessary carry out mouth-to-mouth breathing (and external chest compression if there is no carotid pulse). Check for obvious bleeding (see page 44).
>
> **4** Place the person in the recovery position.
>
> **5** Assess the level of responsiveness – check and note every 10 minutes.
>
> **6** Obtain medical help.

Let us look at an example. Imagine that you are working in a hotel kitchen, it is very hot and suddenly one of the kitchen porters slumps to the floor apparently in a faint.

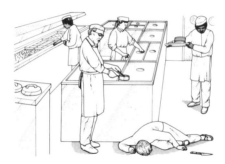

*Fig. 27*

*What should you do?*

**SAFEGUARD:** There is a sharp knife to be picked up and stored safely (see page 11).

**EXAMINE:** All you know is that he is unconscious.

**EMERGENCY AID:** Remember the ABC procedure:
Open/clear the AIRWAY. If the casualty is breathing place in RECOVERY POSITION.

If the casualty is not breathing carry out mouth-to-mouth breathing (see page 17).

Fainting can occur in a variety of circumstances. Usually there is only a brief loss of consciousness, but whenever you have an unconscious casualty you must check breathing and heartbeat.

**MEDICAL HELP:** Call qualified help as soon as possible.

You can give adequate Emergency Aid to an unconscious casualty without knowing exactly what caused the problems . . . although this information is obviously helpful. The cause of accident might be obvious or there could be clues such as a warning bracelet like this:

*Fig. 28*

*Look at this drawing:*

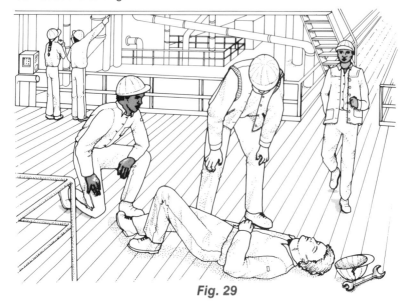

**Fig. 29**

This man has been accidently knocked unconscious, you have carried out stages 1 to 3 of SEEM (ie SAFEGUARD, EXAMINE, EMERGENCY AID), the casualty is breathing normally and there is no bleeding. Having sent for MEDICAL HELP, *what should you do next?*

You should gently roll him into the recovery position (see page 20). If possible you should put some warm dry material on the ground beneath him. If more warm clothes or other items are available, these should be placed over him.

You must stay with him and keep checking his breathing, carotid pulse and level of responsiveness.

**NOTE:**

1  You must never give an unconscious or partly conscious casualty anything to drink, as he may be unable to swallow and fluid may block the airway.
2  Anyone who has been unconscious (even for a very short time) must be sent to a hospital accident and emergency department or be instructed to seek qualified medical help at the workplace or to visit his own doctor.

## Poisoning

If you swallow, inhale or absorb anything through the skin that effects the correct working of the body, then you are **poisoned.**

The EMERGENCY AID is the same, whatever the substance involved – whether tablets, corrosive poison, alcohol, solvents, gases, injections or even snakebites are to blame.

*Your actions are:*

**SAFEGUARD:**      Carefully remove any poisonous substances.

**EXAMINE:**      Ask the casualty or others what happened.

**EMERGENCY AID:**      If the casualty is **unconscious** –

Carry out the standard ABC procedures:

> Check airway and breathing;
> If normal, place in recovery position. If breathing stops then apply **mouth-to-mouth breathing** (BUT if there are dangerous chemicals around the lips which could contaminate the first aider (eg corrosives, cyanide etc) the correct procedure would be to use a manual method of *artificial ventilation* – details of courses where you can learn such technique are on page 67).
> Send for qualified help (but do not leave the casualty alone). Find out as many facts about the situation as you can.

If the casualty is **conscious** –

> Ask what happened (quickly in case he or she becomes unconscious).

**MEDICAL HELP:**      DO NOT make the person vomit.
Send for qualified help.
If there are burns around the lips or mouth give sips of water or milk. Place in the recovery position (although not unconscious the casualty could vomit).

In many industrial processes poisonous chemicals are used. Remember ALWAYS OBEY ANY SAFETY REGULATIONS TO AVOID TURNING YOURSELF INTO ANOTHER CASUALTY.

*Now think about this situation:*
Imagine that you work in an hotel. One evening a man who has been drinking at the bar falls to the ground, breaking the glass.

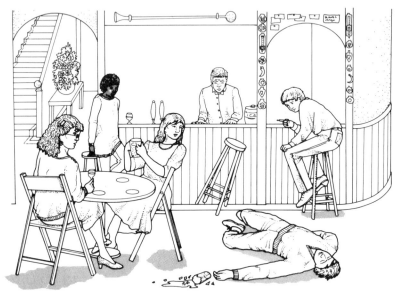

*Fig. 30*

*What should you do?*

**SAFEGUARD:**   Remove the glass quickly.

**EXAMINE:**   He is unconscious but breathing normally.

**EMERGENCY AID:**   Place him in the recovery position. An important point to note is that the alcohol might not be the reason for his unconsciousness.

**MEDICAL HELP:**   Whatever the cause, an unconscious casualty needs medical treatment so get qualified help. In certain medical conditions, such as diabetes, this must be obtained very quickly.

## Epilepsy

In a major epileptic attack a casualty will lose consciousness, fall to the ground, go rigid and then start to jerk violently.

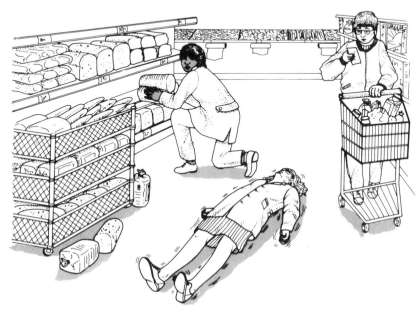

*Fig. 31*

Think about what you should do, based on the standard Emergency Aid for unconsciousness and your own general knowledge . . .

**SAFEGUARD:** You actually should do nothing except safeguard the casualty in the following ways:

Try to protect the person, for example by breaking the fall.
Clear spectators away.

**EXAMINE:** It is likely that the casualty wears a warning locket or bracelet or carries an orange card stating that she is liable to epileptic fits.

**EMERGENCY AID:** If possible, carefully loosen clothing around the neck. When the convulsions stop, place her in the recovery position.

**MEDICAL HELP:** Stay with her until qualified help arrives.
DO NOT try to restrain her.
DO NOT move her unless she is in danger.
DO NOT try to open the mouth or place anything in it (even if the tongue has been bitten).
DO NOT try to rouse her.
DO NOT giving her anything to drink until she is fully alert.

A SUMMARY OF the Emergency Aid for unconsciousness. Remember the ABC procedures:

---

1 Open the airway.

2 Check breathing (see page 15) and heartbeat (see page 27).

3 Examine the casualty quickly for serious injury.

4 Treat any serious bleeding (see page 44).

5 Assess level of responsiveness (and check every ten minutes) (see page 35).

6 Examine the casualty for less serious injury or possible cause of unconsciousness.

7 Place in the recovery position; note – it will be necessary to place the casualty in the recovery position at any time if the airway is likely to be obstructed or vomiting occurs or is likely.

---

Look at this incident:

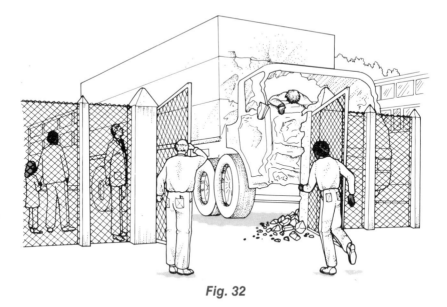

*Fig. 32*

If an unconscious casualty is found in a crashed vehicle, he should be left in the vehicle unless it is absolutely necessary to move him. The only reasons for moving the casualty are the presence of further danger or the need to perform chest compression as shown by the absence of a carotid pulse. You can open the airway in the normal manner, supporting the casualty's head with your hands.

Bleeding is another potential cause of death, but, depending on how bad it is you can probably stop (or at least slow down) the flow. In this chapter you will learn what to do for both external and internal bleeding.

## External bleeding

This can obviously be fairly dramatic (and unpleasant) for both the casualty and you. The treatment, however, is straightforward:

If a wound is bleeding simply press on it with your fingers or squeeze the sides of the cut together maintaining continuous pressure using dressings or pads secured with a bandage. (USE A CLEAN HANDKERCHIEF OR TISSUES OR YOUR FINGERS IF NO DRESSINGS ARE AVAILABLE. DO **NOT** WASTE TIME SEARCHING FOR DRESSINGS). Alternatively, you can tell the casualty to exert this pressure for him or herself. The technique is called "applying direct pressure". You should never apply a tourniquet.

Pressure must be maintained for at least 5 minutes and possibly up to 15 minutes to give the blood time to clot. The dressings or pads that have been secured with a bandage must always be left in place. If necessary, extra dressings should be secured on top.

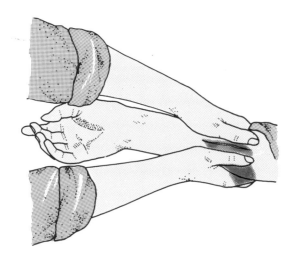

*Fig. 33*

Gravity can be used to reduce the amount of blood flowing out of the wound. Gravity can also be used to help blood flow to the brain and other vital organs. *Have a look at this example:*

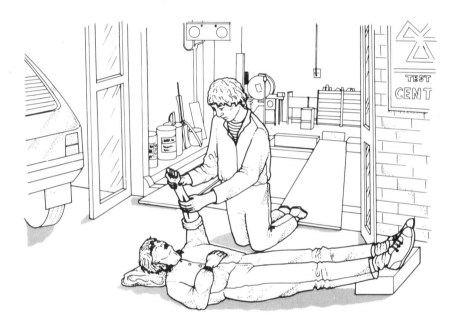

**Fig. 34**

Here the man's arm has been raised to control bleeding – you can do this with any limb provided you do not suspect it is broken. Note that his feet have been raised (see page 50).

Now think carefully about this question:

*If there is a large piece of glass or metal embedded in the wound, should you remove it?*

The answer is "no" unless it is loose because it could actually be helping to block an injured blood vessel – pulling it out could make the bleeding worse. Any object embedded in a wound should be removed only at a hospital.

*EMERGENCY AID for such a wound is:*

1 Squeeze the edges of the wound together alongside the object.

2 Use gravity to help control the flow of blood; lay the casualty down and lift the injured part.

3 Place rolled up dressings on each side of the object. Try to build up a pile of pads so that there is no pressure on the object.

4 Secure the pads firmly with a bandage, diagonally applied to avoid pressure on the object.

5 If the pads become soaked with blood do not remove them. Place fresh pads on top and rebandage firmly.

6 Finally you must arrange for qualified help and inform people as necessary.

The same basic procedure (applying direct pressure and pads) applies to all almost all cases of external bleeding.

When dealing with bleeding, you should be as hygienic as possible, so that infection does not pass to or from the casualty. Whenever possible, wash your hands thoroughly before dealing with wounds, and wash them again (with soap and water) after you have finished. In emergency situations however stopping severe bleeding quickly is more important than cleanliness. Always remember that if the patient is conscious he can help control the bleeding himself.

See how the stages apply to this situation;

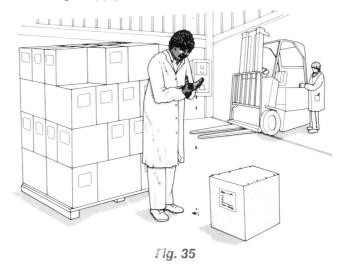

*Fig. 35*

*What should you do?*

**SAFEGUARD:**    In the excitement people might forget standard operating procedures and cause another accident, make sure that the forklift truck is switched off.

**EXAMINE:**    There seems to be a lot of blood – but remember a little blood seems to go a long way.

**EMERGENCY AID:**    Get him to sit down – he will be more comfortable. Instruct him to apply direct pressure to the wound and lift his arm whilst you wash your hands (if possible). Put a pad over the wound and bandage firmly (still keeping up the pressure). He will not be losing enough blood to affect the vital organs but he might faint. If so place him in the recovery position. After you have finished wash your hands with soap and water.

**MEDICAL HELP:**    Carry out the normal accident reporting procedure.

That was a fairly minor accident – but suppose you were present when something really horrifying like this accident occurs.
Would you be able to cope?

*Fig. 36*

Look back at the Emergency Aid for bleeding (page 46) and take a moment or two to work out for yourself how you should apply it in this incident.

**SAFEGUARD:** Make sure that you remove carefully any glass that could injure you or further injure the casualty (*not* glass that is embedded in a wound).

**EXAMINE:** There is a large wound with glass in it on the girl's left arm and another large cut without glass on her leg. She is conscious and has several superficial cuts on her hands.

**EMERGENCY AID:** Raise both limbs and apply direct pressure to both edges of the leg wound whilst a colleague builds pads around the arm wound. Avoid pressure on the glass embedded in it. Bandage firmly. Remember, if blood seeps through the pads, do not remove them, but put more on top.

**MEDICAL HELP:** One of your colleagues should call an ambulance immediately.

*One other important point* about bleeding is that you must still remember to check breathing and heartbeat – they take priority over controlling bleeding.

### Internal bleeding

If a person has been crushed or had a bad fall, then it is possible that internal bleeding will occur (although the effects may not be recognised until some time after the accident).

Internal bleeding causes blood to collect in the body's cavities or muscles. It may eventually come out of one of the body openings (for example the mouth). The danger to the casualty is that blood is lost from the actual circulatory system and so cannot carry oxygen to the brain and other vital organs.

*Fig. 37*

In a situation like this you should not move the casualty unless absolutely necessary (for example to apply external chest compression *or* to place him in the recovery position *or* to remove him and yourself from further danger).

You obviously cannot apply direct pressure so you must just do all you can to minimise shock. Keep checking breathing and pulse.

*Which of these statements would probably describe his pulse?*

**a** Slow and strong
**b** Fast and weak

The pulse would be fast and weak. Fast because the heart would be striving to pump blood to the vital organs and weak because the casualty may have lost a considerable amount of blood.

## Shock

Shock may follow many injuries and is caused when the circulation of the blood fails. This happens when the heart is unable to maintain circulatory pressure (as in heart attacks or electrocution), or the amount of blood in the body is reduced due to external or internal bleeding or to severe burns.

The body reacts by trying to direct blood to the vital organs – eg brain, heart and kidneys, and away from less important areas such as the skin. This will cause the casualty to become pale or even grey in colour and feel cold. As with severe bleeding, the pulse is fast and weak, and if conscious, a casualty is usually weak, faint and anxious. The aim of Emergency Aid is to improve blood supply to the brain, heart and lungs and to arrange urgent removal to hospital.

1 Treat any cause such as external bleeding. Reassure the casualty, but try not to move him unnecessarily.

2 Lay down, head low and to one side to lessen the dangers of vomiting (for the treatment of heart attack see page 62).

3 Raise the legs.

4 Loosen tight clothing round neck, chest and waist.

5 Keep comfortable, and cover with a blanket.

6 Check breathing, pulse and level of responsiveness.

7 If casualty starts to lose consciousness or if breathing becomes difficult, or vomiting is likely, place in the recovery position.

8 Arrange urgent removal to hospital.

In the example below a female employee carrying boxes, has tripped on a stairway and fallen.

**Fig. 38**

**SAFEGUARD:** Remove boxes on stairs to prevent further accidents.

**EXAMINE:** She is conscious, but her pulse is fast and weak.

**EMERGENCY AID:** You tell her to stay lying quietly where she is until qualified help arrives. She says she feels cold.

*Which of the following things would you use to help warm her?* (You can use more than one if you wish).

**a** Electric heater
**b** Blankets over her
**c** Blankets under her
**d** Hot sweet drink

**a** Allow the girl to warm up naturally by placing blankets over her.

**b** Blankets under her would be even more valuable as the body would loose more heat to the ground than to the air. Remember, however, that you must not move a conscious casualty if there is the slightest risk of spinal injuries.

**c** Drinks of any sort MUST NEVER be given to a casualty except in the special cases mentioned elsewhere in this book. You can moisten her lips with water but that is all.

**d** Do not use electric heater, pads, hot water bottles etc since this overheats the skin and blood is diverted to it to cool it, away from vital organs eg the brain.

**MEDICAL HELP:**  A colleague should have sent for qualified help.

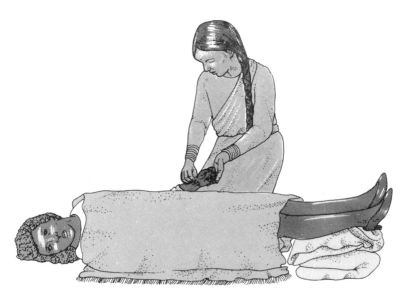

*Fig. 39*

The Emergency Aid for burns and scalds is the same and is based on the simple fact that you need to *cool* the affected area . . . this chapter will tell you what to do.

Let us start by considering a fairly minor incident:

*Fig. 40*

This man has touched a hot exhaust pipe and has a small burn on his hand. *Which of the following is the correct Emergency Aid?*

● Apply a sterile adhesive plaster.
● Put grease on the burn to soothe the pain.
● Do nothing.
● Get him to hold his hand under cold water.

The best Emergency Aid is to hold the hand under cold water for at least 10 minutes to cool the skin. **Do not** cover a burn or scald with an adhesive plaster, grease or ointment.

*Fig. 41*

Whilst you are cooling the injury you should also remove any rings, watches, belts or tight clothing near the burned area, as it will probably swell. **Do not** however remove any clothing that is stuck to the burn.

There are other things that you need to do if the injury is of a different type – here are the types of injury you might meet in your work place.

*Fig. 42*

| | |
|---|---|
| Dry burns: | Caused by heat, for example a flame or a very hot object, or by friction. |
| Scalds: | Caused by wet heat such as steam or hot water. |
| Cold burns: | Caused by contact with a freezing agent or very cold metal. |
| Electrical burns: | Caused by electrical currents or lightning. |
| Chemical burns: | Caused by corrosive chemicals. |

Remember, burns and scalds are often serious injuries. If there is any doubt about the severity of the injury always seek more qualified medical help.

We have looked at one example of a dry burn and given you examples of other causes of burning. We have said that the Emergency Aid is to cool the burned area using cold water and to remove any tight fitting objects or clothing close to the injured part.

If a casualty is scalded or has come into contact with a corrosive chemical it will be necessary, after flooding the area with cold water, to remove any clothing which may be contaminated by the chemical.

When removing the clothing, always take care not to come into contact with the burning agent. Remember, **do not** remove any clothing that is stuck to the burn, **do not** apply any adhesive plaster, or ointment to the burned area and **do not** break any blisters.

We have now covered the general rules for the Emergency Aid treatment of burns and scalds.

*Let us look at an incident which is a little more serious.*

**Fig. 43**

**SAFEGUARD:** The Bunsen Burner has set light to the laboratory coat, you must obviously extinguish the flames, but how?

*Assuming that there is no special fire-fighting equipment available, should you:*

**a** roll him on the ground?
**b** wrap him in a coat or blanket?
**c** throw water over him?

One essential point is that you must make the casualty lie down rather than allowing him to panic and rush about.

You should not roll him on the ground as this might cause the flames to spread.

If you have a bucket of water immediately available then you could use this to put out flames, but you must not waste time trying to find one.

The best answer is probably to wrap him in a coat or blanket (provided that the fabric is not man-made and liable to melt. Do not use a cellular blanket). Subject to those restrictions you should use anything available to smother the flames.

Also the Bunsen Burner needs to be turned off as soon as possible.

**EXAMINE:** The laboratory technician has severe burns to his left hand and right leg.

**EMERGENCY AID:** With the casualty lying down, carefully pour jugs of cold water over the burned area until the pain has stopped.

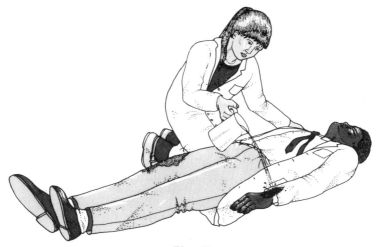

*Fig. 44*

Gently remove anything tight before the injured area starts to swell (BUT do not remove anything which is sticking to a burn).

The next stage is to cover the burn – remembering that you must try to reduce the risk of infection and not cause unnecessary pain. Think about this question:

*What essential features must you look for in anything you intend to use to cover a burn?*

It must be clean and it must not be fluffy (threads might stick to the burn). You could use a clean (preferably new) plastic bag to cover an injured hand or foot.

As with small burns, you must not;

● apply any adhesive plasters, grease, creams or ointments;
● break any blisters;
● remove any loose skin;

You must also:

- minimise the risk of shock (see page 50);
- if the casualty becomes unconscious carry out the ABC procedure (see page 14);

Ideally you should immobilise a badly burnt arm or leg – techniques are taught on the courses mentioned on page 67.

**MEDICAL HELP:** Send a colleague for qualified help at once.

*Now consider this situation:*

*Fig. 45*

**SAFEGUARD:** Put the stopper on the bleach bottle.

**EXAMINE:** An office cleaner has screamed because some bleach has splashed in her eye.

**EMERGENCY AID:** Quickly use cold, gently running water to wash away the chemical. There is an important point to bear in mind about the contaminated water which is running away – it must drain off the face without going anywhere near the good eye.

*Fig. 46*

You must check that both surfaces of the eyelid have been well washed (you may need to help by gently but firmly pulling the eyelids open).

Another method of cleaning the eye is to sit or lay the casualty down with their head tilted back and towards the injured side. Whilst you protect the good side gently open the affected eye and pour clean water over it.

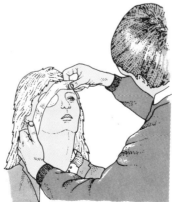

*Fig. 47*

You should now cover the eye with clean, non-fluffy cloth.

It is essential that the casualty does not rub her eye.

SUMMARY of Emergency Aid for severe burns is:

- Make the casualty lie down (try to keep the burned area from contact with the ground).

- Carefully pour jugs of cold water over the burned area until the pain has stopped.

- Gently remove anything tight from the injured area before it starts to swell (BUT do not remove anything which is sticking to a burn).

- Cover the burn – remembering that you must use a clean, non-fluffy cloth. You could use a clean (preferably new) plastic bag to cover an injured hand or foot.

- Immobilise a badly burned arm or leg with pillows or other soft materials.

- If breathing stops, then immediately apply the ABC procedure (see Chapters 2, 3 and 4).

If a casualty has a foreign object in the eye then you should follow almost the procedure outlined on page 59. The difference is that, if the object is not stuck or embedded or on the coloured part of the eye and does not wash away, you can lift it off with, for example the corner of a clean, dampened handkerchief. If the object does not come off, then cover the eye with a non-fluffy pad and seek medical help.

This book cannot teach you how to deal with all major injuries. If you want to learn how to do those things you need to attend one of the courses mentioned on page 67.

In fact, the main emergency aid that you can provide for someone with a bone, joint or muscle problem is to keep the person still and steady (particularly if you suspect a broken bone), support the injured limb and to guard against shock. Do not try to do too much, send for more qualified help.

If you are certain that the casualty has injured soft tissue (such as a muscle) rather than a bone (in other words, if they have a strain or sprain) you could use the following treatment: (Note that to help you remember the initial letters spell RICE)

**R** – Rest the injured part in the most comfortable position. Apply an
**I** – Icebag (wrapped in a towel) or cold-water compress for at least 30 minutes.
**C** – Compress the injury with a thick layer of cotton wool secured with a firm bandage.
**E** – Elevate (raise) the injured limb.

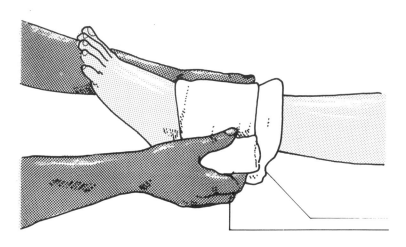

*Fig. 48*

It is essential that if someone is taken seriously ill you can provide the correct Emergency Aid until medical help arrives.

You have already seen how to cope with problems caused by epilepsy (pages 41 and 42). Now we are going to consider the most common cause of death in this country, heart attack.

## Heart attack

There are various medical problems under this heading but the Emergency Aid you should provide is the same. First, however, how do you know if a casualty is having a heart attack?

*Typical signs and symptoms are:*

> **1** That there is severe pain in the chest (or even in the stomach) which does not go away when the person rests;
>
> **2** the skin may be ashen and the lips blue;
>
> **3** the person may be short of breath;
>
> **4** sweating may develop;
>
> **5** the pulse may be fast and become weaker and irregular;
>
> **6** there may be symptoms of shock (page 47).

In addition the casualty may become unconscious and breathing and heart beat might stop.

**BE WARNED** – a heart attack sometimes seems to mimic other conditions, such as indigestion. Some of the signs and symptoms might not occur.

A Cardiac Arrest (where the heart actually stops beating) is obviously a most serious emergency. The ABC procedure must be used immediately (see page 14). If there is no carotid pulse then you must carry out external chest compression along with mouth-to-mouth breathing. (See page 17.)

*If there is a faint or irregular pulse, do you think you should carry out external chest compression?*

No. You must not carry out external chest compression if the casualty's heart is beating.

The correct Emergency Aid where the heart has not stopped and the casualty is conscious is as follows:

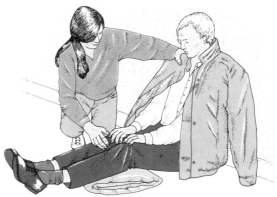

*Fig. 49*

Help him to sit (give him support by placing something like a jacket or blanket under the knees).

Loosen any tight clothing round the neck, chest and waist.

If he becomes unconscious but is breathing normally you should place him in the recovery position.

If his breathing and heartbeat stop, apply mouth-to-mouth breathing and carry out external chest compression.

The casualty must be removed to hospital as soon as possible and you must inform people as necessary (see page 11).

## Angina pectoris (pain in the chest)

This is usually brought on by exercise or excitement, the attacks normally last only a few minutes. The person may have previously seen a doctor and know how to cope – for example by resting and/or taking special tablets.

## Strokes

These are also caused by circulation difficulties but the problem is in the brain rather than the heart.

*Typical signs and symptoms are:*

> **1** Possible sudden, severe headache or giddiness;
>
> **2** A strong pulse;
>
> **3** The casualty might be disorientated, confused, frightened or crying;
>
> **4** A progressive loss of consciousness;
>
> **5** Muscular weakness or paralysis.

The Emergency Aid you should provide if the casualty is conscious is: lay him down with head and shoulders slightly raised and supported; lean the head to one side (so that saliva can drain out of the mouth) loosen any tight clothing around the neck, chest and waist to assist circulation and breathing.

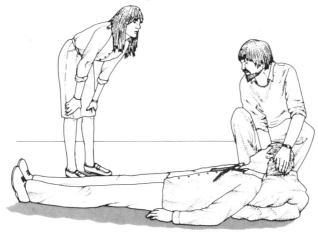

*Fig. 50*

If he becomes unconscious then you must carry out the ABC of resuscitation: open the airway, apply mouth-to-mouth breathing and give external chest compression if necessary or, if he is breathing, place him in the recovery position.

He must go to hospital as soon as possible and then you have to inform people as necessary (see page 11).

There is one important point for stroke or heart attack casualties – do not give them anything to eat or drink.

In this book we have looked at various situations where, basically by using common sense, you might save someone's life or keep them from a more serious injury. You have seen that there are four things to think about at any incident:

**SAFEGUARD**

**EXAMINE**          remember as

**EMERGENCY AID**      **SEEM**

**MEDICAL HELP**

Over the next few pages you will find some more useful information but first look at these general points about Emergency Aid:

Always check Airway, Breathing and Circulation (ABC procedure), whatever other injuries the casualty has.

Never move someone with possible neck or spinal injuries unless you have to apply mouth-to-mouth breathing and if necessary given external chest compression or unless the casualty is in a dangerous position – fire or other danger or complicating injuries eg an unconscious casualty left lying on his back and at risk of inhaling vomit.

Always send the casualty to hospital if you think that there are internal injuries or if the person has been unconscious.

Finally, decide whether you should attend a course to practice the procedures in this book, learn more and to become a qualified First Aider.

## First aid equipment

If, in terms of the Health and Safety (First Aid) Regulations 1981, you are named by your employer as an Appointed Person, you will be expected to take charge of the situation (for example to call an ambulance) if a serious injury or major illness occurs, if the First-Aider is absent or where it is not required by law for one to be appointed.

In such circumstances, the Appointed Person is also responsible for ensuring the contents of the First Aid boxes, supplied by the employer, are in accordance with the items and quantities shown in the Health and Safety Executive. Approved Code of Practice which states First Aid boxes should contain a sufficient amount of suitable First Aid materials AND NOTHING ELSE – in most cases this will be.

| ITEM | |
|---|---|
| Guidance Card | 1 |
| Individual wrapped sterile adhesive dressings | 20 |
| Sterile eye pads, with attachment | 2 |
| Triangular bandages | 6 |
| Safety pins | 6 |
| Medium-sized sterile unmedicated dressings | 6 |
| Large sterile unmedicated dressings | 3 |
| Extra large sterile unmedicated dressings | 2 |
| Where sterile water or sterile normal saline in disposable containers needs to be kept near the first aid box because tap water is not available, at least the following quantities should be kept: | |
| Sterile water or normal saline in disposable containers (where tap water is not available) | 3×300 ml containers |

This book has given you guidance on what to do if you are at the scene of an accident.

Throughout, the book emphasises that there is no real substitute for a proper First Aid training course. Remember, Mouth-to-Mouth Breathing and External Chest Compression must only be practised under qualified supervision. To enable you to practise these skills and also gain greater knowledge of First Aid, St John Ambulance Association runs the following courses:

### Emergency Aid (Appointed Persons) Course
This is a 4 hour course which gives practical training in mouth- to-mouth breathing, external chest compression and it is based on the contents of this book.

### Community First Aid (Basic) Course
This is an 8 hour course which gives the student a basic knowledge of first aid including practical training in mouth-to-mouth breathing and external chest compression, the treatment of the unconscious casualty and wounds and bleeding. A certificate, valid for three years, is issued.

### Public First Aid Course
This is a 16 hour course which gives a student greater knowledge of First Aid. A certificate, valid for three years, is issued.

### First Aid at Work Course
This is a 24 hour course which leads to the issue of a statutory First Aid at Work certificate recognised for the purposes of the Health and Safety (First Aid) Regulations 1981.

Details of all St John Ambulance courses are available from your local County offices (see useful addresses appended).

*The address of St John Ambulance Headquarters is:*

1 Grosvenor Crescent
London
SW1X 7EF

Tel: 071–235–5231

# County Branches of St John Ambulance Association

| COUNTY | ADDRESS | TELEPHONE No. |
|---|---|---|
| AVON | 10 Woodborough St., Easton, Bristol | 0272 512567 |
| BEDFORDSHIRE | 34 St John's St., Bedford | 0234 216200 |
| BERKSHIRE | 101 London Rd., Reading | 0734 574671 |
| BUCKINGHAMSHIRE | Croft Rd., Aylesbury | 0296 23886 |
| CAMBRIDGESHIRE | 3 Barton Rd., Cambridge | 0223 355334 |
| CHESHIRE | 142 Foregate St., Chester | 02443 344878 |
| CLEVELAND | 11 Cornfield Rd., Middlesbrough | 0642 826723 |
| CORNWALL | The Training Centre, Par Moor Rd., Par | 0726 815967 |
| CUMBRIA | Scalegate Rd., Upperby, Carlisle | 0228 28684 |
| DERBYSHIRE | Alma House, Derby Rd., Chesterfield | 0246 200272 |
| DEVON | Tamar Ward, Langdon Hosp., Exeter Rd., Dawlish | 0626 888359 |
| DORSET | North Square, Dorchester | 0305 64510 |
| DURHAM | 27 Old Elvet, Durham | 091 3869062 |
| ESSEX | Lancaster Ho., 140 Mildmay Rd., Chelmsford | 0245 265678 |
| GLOUCESTERSHIRE | 12 Royal Cres., Cheltenham | 0242 513610 |
| Gtr MANCHESTER | Egerton Ho., Fallowfield | 061 2252764 |
| GUERNSEY | Headquarters, Rohais, St Peter Port | 0481 27129 |
| HAMPSHIRE | Worthy La., Winchester | 0962 63366 |
| HERE & WORCS | 148 Wylds La., Worcester | 0905 359512 |
| HERTFORDSHIRE | 102 Ashley Rd., St Albans | 0727 54333 |
| HUMBERSIDE | Priory Ho., Popple Street, Hull HU9 1LP | 0482 588564 |
| ISLE OF MAN | 57 Cronk-ny-Greiney, Tromode Park, Douglas | 0642 26232 |
| ISLE OF WIGHT | Mill Square, Wootton Bridge | 0983 882586 |
| JERSEY | Midvale Rd., St Helier | 0534 35611 |
| KENT | Violet Astor Ho., 41 Church St., Maidstone | 0622 55924 |
| LANCASHIRE | 15–17 Mount St., Preston | 0772 52239 |
| LEICESTERSHIRE | 112 Regent Rd., Leicester | 0533 553954 |
| LINCOLNSHIRE | The Cardinal's Hat, 268 High St., Lincoln | 0522 23701 |
| Gtr LONDON | Edwina Mountbatten Ho., 63 York St., W1 | 071 258 3456 |
| MERSEYSIDE | St Margaret's Parish Ctre, Belmont Rd., Anfield | 051 263 7300 |
| NORFOLK | 59 King St., Norwich | 0603 621649 |
| NORTHANTS | 33a Billing Rd., Northampton | 0604 33711 |
| NORTHUMBRIA | Grainger Park Rd., Newcastle upon Tyne | 091 2737938 |
| N YORKSHIRE | 46 Topcliffe Rd., Sowerby, Thirsk | 0845 22818 |
| NOTTINGHAMSHIRE | 561 Valley Rd., Basford | 0602 784625 |
| OXFORDSHIRE | High St., Kidlington | 086 75–78228 |
| SHROPSHIRE | Priory Rd., Shrewsbury | 0743 231280 |
| SOMERSET | 60 Staplegrove Rd., Taunton | 0823 337285 |
| S & W YORKSHIRE | Garden St., Ravensthorpe, Dewsbury | 0924 497012 |
| STAFFORDSHIRE | 1 Shrewsbury Rd., Stafford | 0785 57124/5 |
| SUFFOLK | 19 Tower St., Ipswich | 0473 54005 |
| SURREY | Stocton Rd., Guildford | 0483 34452 |
| SUSSEX | 25a Farncombe Rd., Worthing | 0903 35599 |
| WARWICKSHIRE | National Agricultural Centre, Stoneleigh | 0203 696521 |
| W MIDLANDS | Nelson Memorial Hall, 100 Lionel St., B'ham | 021 236 6660 |
| WILTSHIRE | St John St., Devizes | 0380 728362 |
| WALES | Priory Ho., Lisvane Rd., Llanishen, Cardiff | 0222 750222 |
| N IRELAND | Erne Purdysburn Hosp., Saintfield Rd., Belfast | 0232 799393 |

# NOTES